The Slip Under My Church Dress

J.W. Bella

J.W. Bella

ISBN: 978-1-970135-19-0 (paperback)
        978-1-970135-20-6 (ebook)

Published in the United States by Pen2Pad Ink Publishing.

Requests to publish work from this book or to contact the author should be sent to: jwbellawrites@gmail.com

Sandrella Bush retains the rights to all images

Interior design: Pen2Pad Ink Publishing

J.W. Bella

Contents

Part 3: The Epiphany

Dedication

You are my blessing and my curse. You have given me so many victories, yet I have suffered numerous defeats due to your arrogance and pride. I lovingly hate you for many reasons, but I am doing my best to live without you.

One day…it just may happen…

The Slip Under My Church Dress

I'm the perfection fixer your outfit never
wants the world to see.
My relationship with your curves keeps me
hanging on.
It keeps me drenched in your body's spell.
But I can't live on touch alone.
Plus…I bore easily.
I desire a new set of hills and valleys to
explore.

Every Sunday, I sit on this almond colored
rose covered bench.
A voice vibrates against the wood telling
me to find some person named God to save
me from something called "sins".
Are those the things I've heard lips reveal
about being a friend while you hold a
dagger to their back?
Maybe it's when I came off in the men's
restroom so you could reach his penis
faster…but your boyfriend's voice called
for you six times?
Or is it your many visits to the payday loan

place to borrow from Peter to show Paul,
Dick, and Harry how you are "balling out
of control"?
If this is sin, I want to know more.
I long for more.
It seems to be the only place where the
truth lives similar to my own lifestyle.

I get annoyed that I cannot be revealed to
the world.
I'm the reason you look immaculate.
I look like silk armor ready to battle
Victoria's Secrets.
You tell the world that your body woke up
like this.
When spotlights beams brightly on you, it
burns my delicate and fragile fabric.

I'm constantly having to adhere to
commands of your over garments and your
mind's corrupted perfection.
A-line, Sheath, or Tunic…take your pick.
Adversity, Slander, and Trickery…make
me sick.
So stand among your admirers.
I will slide down your leg. It's my turn to
be seen. Let me have my moment to shine!
My beige strap looks for land beyond your

shoulders to prove that I will NOT be
ignored.
You will listen to me.
You will reveal truth.

A Mother's Try
Part 1

She is trying.
Like a kid in a candy store
engulfing sweet tarts,
She desires to suck in the sweet positivity
and break down the negativity
with her teeth-
Those calcium developed gods that
protect her tongue from her own stupidity.
Because when the Old Milwaukee tastes
her lips, rapes her mouth, and desensitizes
her ample sense, she fails.
And she fails a lot.

Falling for each male that simply says hi
due to the absence of a
present pastoral patriarch,
She wants the superhero-
S on his chest,
Able to leap tall buildings,
Is it a bird? Is it a plane? NO!
It's Mediocrity giving her the right to settle
because his words are superbly sincere,
and her vagina is willing to work for

whatever will he has printed
for her services rendered:

"I, Mediocrity, leave you millions of painful
inheritances in a disTrust that can only be
given to you after I have completely
screwed over any other man's chance of
being loyal, dedicated, and consistent."

And when Mediocrity leaves disTrust is
inherited along with the final stipulation: a
generational curse of cacophonic chaos. Her
uterus brews toiled eggs mixed with
trouble semen in a cauldron that doubles as
her stomach.

Nine months later…you came.

God's angels trembled.
They never knew someone as beautiful as
you could come from Hell's kitchen.
They never knew this rose would come
from this crooked concrete.
They said, "We HAVE to let her know."
They stormed the front gates of the
street paved with gold,
Bulldozed through every sphere
of earth's protection,

GPS her house,
Infiltrated her dream's ranks like SEAL
team Six to simply say
"You...you have black girl magic brewing
in your womb...
you have someone who will become the
new element next to earth, wind, and fire...
you have someone who will surpass
everything you could think of and
more...we know...
we know the curse scares you...
but your child's greatness...
that greatness blows away darkness like
sunshine on early Sunday morning."

When she woke up, Budweiser was staring
her in the face with the morning after glow.
She sat up and realized "I can do better."
And she did.

A Mother's Try
Part 2

She is trying.
Like JFK attempting to ride down 35 with
the top down,
Destiny comes in the form of danger, but
Lee Harvey Oswald can't take the rap.
She woke up deciding to let go of her lover
Alcohol, but Alcohol clearly believed in
Mariah's words "We Belong Together".

So Alcohol saw fit to put her in the dating
game.
Bachelor 1: A married guy whose days
were spent providing for his family but
nights were spent in creeping in and out
her bed.
Bachelor 2: A crackhead whose hobbies
included riding the same raggedy bike to
match his raggedy pants in order to help
his raggedy habit.
Bachelor 3: A chain smoker imprisoned in
his own illusion of teenage years through
braided hair and basketball jersey shirts.

Yeah...those are some great choices.
For her, they were perfect.
Each one gave her an extraneous gift
wrapped in aluminum foil.
Eventually, they started to stink.
But she was enamored by their words
dripping with disdain and deception so she
fed on every leftover like a pregnant
woman on pickles and ice cream.

Her daughter, however, knew foul smells.
Her nose was new, pristine, and honest.
Bruce Banner gave way to the Incredible
Hulk as daughter lashed out with dagger
infested words and trigger happy actions.
Mother knew.
She knew her daughter's radar was more
updated than Apple iPhones, but Alcohol
kept mother's true words from being
spoken by concealing them in tape made of
self-centered sealant and roughneck
reasoning.

A Mother's Try
Part 3

She is trying.
Like a paternity test on Maury,
Denial and Accusation sit on stage,
but Fear and Embarrassment whine and cry
to the back of the studio.
Because daughter is the audience
of her show.

And daughter doesn't approve.

Mother desires the spirit of morning
sickness: the inability to
control bullshit coming up.
She wants to say all that needs to be
said to her daughter-
The constant need to pee and to release the
toxins floating within her.

But she can't.

She can't admit she is infected.
She needs to be quarantined.
She needs treatment.

For years, the disease has been trickled
down slowly into the birth canal in order to
produce women like her:
women who don't know their worth
because no sense was paid.
Her daughter's jaded daggers continue to
stab her consistently.
Daughter recounts the endless hours of
insomnia caused by the moaning
and groaning of different males
in the next room,
The one way ticket flight from the sofa to
the floor aboard Fake Stepdad Airlines,
The sight of her mother playing a very
convincing punching bag to a drunk
boyfriend's boxing career.
Mother forgot to bring her gun and ammo
to this knife fight.
So daughter's cuts are deeper than Erykah
Badu's window seat.
And…instead of saying sorry…
she remembers that she has one shield
that will never leave her alone: selfishness.

Home

I stayed home.
Heat radiated from granny's mouth
And granny's house.
Unbearable.

I stayed home.

My own land of Mickey and Minnie Mouse
existed,
On my walls,
On my tent,
On my bed.
Uncomfort and chaos awaited me,
Once my toe touched the porch's hot
stovetop.

I stayed home.

Home was supposed to be mom and me.
Two chocolate M & Ms that were nutty,
Hoping we could survive for lifetimes,
Away from taste buds of consumers.
Not possible.
My mom loved the tongue of many who
looked like they wanted a taste.

They begged for indulgence.
She obliged.
Words gnawed softly at her delicate
coating.
This was the key into our home.

I stayed home.
They stayed too.
I convinced myself.
They loved me too.

One night I implored to stay home,
Away from granny's heater house.
Mom said yes.

I stayed home.

Darkness was my most contingent fear.
Night was my worst enemy.
So I asked Consumer
To sleep on the floor of my mom's
bedroom.
Consumer said yes.
I laid down watching TV.
Consumer's Marlboro and Budweiser
breath
Was more than my nostrils could ingest,
But I was more afraid of darkness

So I stayed on floor side.
Plugging my nose with tissue paper to
combat the tobacco demons,
When my breathing became short,
My mouth became a desert,
I balled up the paper and threw it at
Consumer,
My weapon of consumer destruction.
"Stop."
"I told you stop."
"You got one more time."

Consumer's words bounced off of me.
Actions bounced on me.
I stayed home.

Arms shackled me.
I stayed home.

Legs straddle me.
I stayed home.

Chest suppressed me.
I stayed home.

Breath sedated me.
I stayed home.

Hands pinned me.
"Stop. Or this will get worse."
Consumer lingered. Eyes scanned me like a
barcode.

Time stopped.

I stayed home.
Eyes crept into my dreams and made them
nightmares.
My bed became the salad bowl of my
tossing and turning,
Mixed by night's fork and Consumer's
spoon.
Tears welcomed me the next morning to a
new day.
My mom's voice responds.
"What happened?" She said.
I responded.
She replied, "Sounds like your fault. And
your problem."

Home.
I stayed home.
Home betrayed me.
I separated from home just to become me.
Now…I just stay.

Possibilities

Your jail cell was your humble abode.
The bars were your picket fence.
The bed was your wife and
the toilet the perfect pet.
Why would anyone dream of leaving
somewhere so perfect?
Stealing cars and 18 wheelers were the key,
To unlocking your humble residence.
Maids in uniform fed you three times a day.
You had a set time where you could play.
Ah…the joys of such of a harrowing
household.

Meanwhile…

My house was Kansas.
I was Dorothy.
Tornadoes in the form of inadequate men
tore through my mother's farm.
Each ripped a part of her courage,
her emotions, and her intelligence away.
You refused to protect our land.
I dreamed of OZ.
I longed for a place where the yellow brick
road would lead to someone who could

23

make things normal again.
I could ease down a road of hardships,
but three companions would be
fighting with me.
In the end, we would realize that
everything we need was inside
of us all the time.
THAT never happened.

I don't know what my life
could have been with you.
I know what happened without you.
Either way, I'm at a crossroads
that requires me to continuously
click my heels to get back to normal.
But regardless of the medication I consume,
OR the therapy I attend,
I'll never be whole.
I'll always be searching for
what I could not find in you or her.
I'll never be the same.

Three Kings

Brown shoes.
Brown square toe shoes across a wood clad
floor.
Steps are rhythmic and sound.
I want it to be him — the one for whom my
world jumps up and down in anticipation.
Instead my world circles faster than I can
breathe.
My heart goes into cardiac arrest--Charged
with abuse and complicated batteries.
The cuffs on my veins are tight and
restrictive to the circulation to my brain and
my soul.
So my body stops…waiting for the straight
line and time of death.

Tony! Toni! Tone! makes me cry for you.
I see your bedroom.
Junk filled and looking to hire a maid to
deal with your mess…and your mess.
I tell myself I am perfect for the job--put in
my two week notice and all…only to find
out I've been fired before finishing my
application.
You already had many others apply before

I could submit a two week notice.
Were you planning to pay me in pain and
give me a raise of despair?
If so, you earned your promotion to single
life.

How's North Carolina?
Panthers winning?
Tobacco growing?
Finding solace in the civil war
reenactments?
I guess those are battles you can handle.
Was I a war that you wanted to call a
conflict so that people would think it was
unimportant?
Your ammunition of crack, cocaine, and
women couldn't tear down my barriers to
infiltrate my forts of adoration and
comfort?
I would love to report that 6 years of a civil
war is enough for me to concede victory.
But…it's not.
I'm armed with anger, regret, bitterness,
awkwardness, confusion, pain,
disappointment, and unchecked rage.
My cannons stay ready.

My dissertation of madification only

surfaces when degradation encompasses
my complication of rationalization.
(My anger shows up when I'm pissed.)
And sadly, gentlemen, your faces appear in
my head more than Kim Kardashian in Ray
J's bed.

But no matter how many times I rub the
lamp while clicking my heels three times
before midnight, you will never disappear
from the fabric of my magic carpet where
my ruby red slippers reside under my
beautiful blue dress.
Your tattoos are in the worst place possible:
my heart.

He Is Yours

He is your favorite plush toy to hug at 2:19 AM when *Monsters Inc.* earns its energy to supplement their city.

He is your favorite Christmas present that is attached to your hip all day through breakfast, lunch, dinner, Macy's Christmas parade, 3 football games, and the abundance of those aunts that have to kiss you with ruby red lipstick and cigarette breath.

He is your favorite store in the mall that is always open, every pair of skinny jeans is a snug fit, and the price is always right by being 70% off.

He is your favorite song that is on repeat after you hear it the first time and cannot get enough of it because the words speak to your ears and tell your heart all the possibilities of happiness this melody can give your life forever.

He was the same for me. Except…

He was the constant headache that river danced across my dreams and was never off beat with a single step because he knew his routine perfectly.
He was the one thorn the florist could never find in the rose because he hid so perfectly while the other thorns shouted and screamed to be released from their confinement to just one flower.

He was the run in a perfect pair of stockings that morning, but between home and church he came in contact with something that was destined to make the rest of Sunday service hard for me to endure.

He was the 3 week old milk sitting in the refrigerator silently but smelling horribly amongst the fruits, vegetables, and red Kool-Aid because he was waiting for someone to take him out instead of moving on his own.
But I'm sure he is not this way with you.
He is yours.
And while I was stuck with the Apple IPhone 4 version,
He chose to upgrade all his setting and

systems to make himself prepared for
everything you could provide.
All of your compassion.
  Your time.
  Your adoration.

I'm guessing…of course.
But when you lose that toy,
And December 26 rolls around,
Will that store still be open after the music
stops and real life begins?

There's ALWAYS no Wings with You

You fucked me.
Yep. That's it. It's official.
You did it.
Protection was warned but worn.
Trust was given but not received.
Lubrication was not a part of the
manufacturer's system so it was rough
and cruel.
I saw little red dots slowly creep out of the
pink flaps of my friendship vagina.
And it's nowhere near my period.
Each dot of blood cries
a recollection of you.
"I can't be friends with an ex."
"You are one of my few girls that's
actually my friend."
"I will never forget you."
"You're like the girl version of me."
Maxi padding your every word helps me to
soak up your blue liquid and remain
patient until it is time for me to ask a
teacher if I can go to the restroom and bring
my purse with me.

Alone in a stall.
Drawn penises, bitches,
and hoes are etched across the door.
They jump to my heart and carve
themselves into the opening that once
held your beautiful pain.
Fumbling hands make it hard
for me to change.
To forget.
To forfeit.
There I sit...bleeding everywhere...
Because I have no maximum
protection or wings.

A Closet

You was always hidden
Sunday suit soldiers guarded your mystery
Chair and box tanks shielded your secrets
I laid me down to sleep many nights
wondering
> Who are you?
> What's in you?
> Why will I never know the truth
> behind you?
> Did you hold monsters? Lions?
> Tigers? Bears?
> Were you a passage to a world of
> talking lions and satyrs?

My curiosity was not fueled by you alone.

Your queen, a dictative majesty, aided in
fueling the fire between my ears.
She had boxes upon boxes full of
timestamps and memories in the form of
antique mail and ancient photos.
Not once did she reveal the reason or
rhyme to her kingdom,
And her required subject could never
answer.
But when the sun decided to set on her and

she started her eternal rest,
I had the dreaded honor of investigating
the nooks and crannies of her palace.
I understood why her lips never parted,
To bring my knowledge and suspicion
together in harmony,
And Lewinsky's skirt cried in terror,
Her biggest scandal was truth:

>The fact that she was queen by
>default.
>The fact that she lied.
>The fact that she deceived.
>The fact that she hoarded.
>The fact she feared her subjects more
>than she feared knights with sharp
>swords and bloodshot eyes.

As I tore through each truth,
Tears tore my heart open,
Taking time to grip each emotional vein,
And yank until completely severed.
Then, I remembered you.
Your soldiers were powerless now,
>Tanks ammo less.
I was ready to win the battle,
And find out your internal treasures.

My hands became boat fins.

I propelled through each box

Left

  Right

Left

  Right go cardboard and clothes.
Fling the chair like a discus of the
Olympiads.
Pull each suit down from its post.
And there you are,
Naked.
Unlocked.
Available to me.
The knob turns.
Light seeps in to vacant spaces.

I find...nothing.

You are bare with stale oxygen occupying
your body.
But how?
How can the rest of this fortress hold truth
and honesty,
And you have nothing to give?
I slept many nights wondering of your
content.
I passed you on the way to the bathroom

and kitchen knowing your stored treasure
and fulfillment.
Yet...nothing.

Click.

I realized in that moment that was your
purpose.
While the world around you was so busy
attempting to
      hide
            conceal
                  shadow
                        divert,
You were here
      empty
            honest
                  transparent
                        true.
You hid nothing.
    had no secrets.
    reminded me that I don't have to have
    secrets.

I don't have to hide.
I don't have to be busy.
I can be empty,
And still be full.

The Proper Black Girl of Crowley Instructions

Come here.
Let me instruct you on the proper way to be
black in Crowley.
Lil' mama, I will school you on the
importance of Ebonics happiness in
housing authority dreams.
You desiring and wanting more is a fantasy
Mariah Carey cannot congeal into a musical
masterpiece.
Your idea: It's ok to say "you all" and the
ends of words.
You can call the police, and someone will
come.
Sweetheart that is not your job.
Your job consists of twisting your hips in
tight booty shorts up and down Hutchinson
Avenue.
You smile prettily at all the low riders that
stop to admire your physique and beg for
some time alone between your cheeks.
You are not smart.
You are gullible.
Your legs open wide for any and every boy

or man who speaks those magic words to open your broken treasure chest "Baby, I ain't going anywhere. I'm yours".
It is not your job to respect your elders or your teachers.
Your job is make them earn their keep if they want to be a part of your life.
You breathe hell in those classrooms.
Roll every single bone in your neck when someone tries to correct you, and live your life within the confines of detention or out of school suspension.
Your friends are girls who are like you: messy and simple.
The hair on their head is far more important than the grey matter in their skull, and the money spent on it could rival the US debt amount.
Spend thousands on expensive shoes and clothes to appear like you are "ballin' out of control".
Rip the shit out of little girls who act smart and like they are better than everyone else.
You are black.
You are a girl.
You in Crowley.
That's your job.

A Lady's Lie

Sometimes I say I'm going to go home to
Crowley —
     even though I despise its existence.
I see so many humans whose hearts are at
home.

I never understood —
     how joy found their mouths and
hearts.
Red blood on my doorpost must have cued
passing me over.

I received a message asking if I intended on
reuniting with my graduating class.
I started to laugh.
I remembered some people enjoyed high
school, but none of those people were me.
I was the black sheep that wished to never
run in that pasture again.
I replied "No".
Her response of "Oh" informed me I was
no longer of interest anymore.

I desire comfort.
I desire a gavel free zone so judgment

cannot exist.
I desire a place where unique is the store
name, and I can fit any size clothes.

It is not Crowley.
It's not the place where racism is black and
white.
It's not the place that made me say yes in
order to be accepted.

I scroll through Facebook timelines wishing
I could say I'm friends with those I grew up
with.
Marriages and babies bless the population
but condense my heart to pieces.
These pieces saturate my blood stream so
they can travel all over my body.

They remind me that I am alone.
I am lonely for a home.

Lula Farris

The nerve of you.
To be confident,
To be honest,
To be beautiful,
When your body said otherwise.

The nerve of you.
To be melodic,
To be sane,
To be supportive,
When your body didn't believe.

The nerve of you.
To be instinctive,
To be fair,
To be majestic,
When your body gave in.

The nerve of you.
To be sensible,
To be God-fearing,
To be caring,
When your body transitioned beyond.

The nerve of you.

To be real,
To be truthful,
To be forward thinking,
When your body is no longer present.

The nerve of you after all these years to
still have an imprint on my heart.

THE JOURNEY

Taken

A ransom note tattooed the mirror's chest.
Words leaked in blood straddled the curves
of the paper.
My eyes widened soccer ball size.
My heart and feet became roommates.
Somewhere in a dark room or lone cabin is
my sanity.

I can imagine her:
Small wrists cuffed in silver metal
Linked together with no signs of release
or avail.
She wiggles profusely.
Her eyes release water droplets.
Her face secretes sweat in buckets.
Her mind racing down tracks with Daytona
500 crowds.
She tries to find comfort on the hard brown
chair
Comfort needs to last a while.

I…I can't get to her.
Payday loans, medical bills, maxed out
credit cards, and old bad decisions paper
the walls.

Headlines are numbers filled with commas.
Minus is the plus equaling the sum of all
my fears:
I may not have the time or funding to
rescue her and bring her back home.

I desire God's grace and work in the plan.
His leadership will I ever follow.
Worry wearies me to dreams and
distractions.
I can't give HIM the room to operate
    where anxiety and distrust run amuck.

So I sink behind the sink.
Slide to the floor of my bathroom.
I know my sanity is gone —
    for an indefinite time period.

Multi-tasking

My safety rope cannot handle this.
Sturdy clasps are loosened knots that
slowly and unwillingly drop me out of
Sky's grace into Earth's bosom.
And she decided today of all days to go
without her support bra.
So falling I am over student test papers,
grad school assignments, parental concerns,
identity crises, heightened expectations,
ridiculous grades, friends' problems,
money complications, family fights, and
household deaths.
My parachute wants to play hooky today of
all days.
I try to hold on to the rock
        My short hands fail to stretch.
I extend for the branch
        Its shady ass bends and breaks
        under pressure.
I pray to the wind to carry me beneath its
wings
        The wind howls with laughter as it
        tries to paint with all colors.
So I brace myself for the impact: the
acceptance of the truth I've never been able

to fathom or string along.
I've not made for this type of feat. I found a
mountain that I cannot turn into a molehill.
5 inches...
I'm not a multitasker.
4...
I can't help everyone.
3...
I'm not meant for this.
2...
That's the way it is.
1...
I fear what the sky has in store for me.

Life's Featured Attraction

It's not as simple as high then low.
Up then down.
Elated then Depressed.

It's not just a rollercoaster ride that only has
all mountains then straight valleys.
Twist then turns.
Straight-a-ways then loops.

It's my heart and my mind in a constant tug
of war as to who gets me
in the custody battle.
My heart has been there.
Nights when I cried consistently and
overflowed the Nile River not with
water...but with unfulfilled love.
My mind made me.
It formed me with clay of logic,
shaped me with tools of sense, and
taught me that reasoning is life.

So when I strap into the rollercoaster my
Excitement warns me

The Slip Under My Church Dress

This ride is going to be longer than you thought.
You are not ready for this.
I shrug her off and check
my Sanity's seat belt.
But Excitement was right.
I am not ready for this.

The car creaks up the mountain.
Each click is a fun memory.
Each clack is horror warmed up.
The top of the rollercoaster mountain sees
me, knows I'm alone, and could care less.
My heart and my mind are too busy
fighting a battle that has no winner.
I drop hopelessly...screaming with no voice.

So it's not as simple as high then low.
Up then down.
Elated then Depressed.
It's my life
and you have to be THIS strong
then tall to ride.

Shame

Doused in gasoline and set on fire
Because she is different
> black with a white voice
> quiet but loud at the wrong time
> a useful tool but still in the box
> an unstable boulder teetering on a
plateau's nose
> a queen trapped in a jester's suit
> a bridesmaid's fake tears of
happiness for the
bride
> an unnecessary key change in a
choral
singing

Invisible brands engulf her face
Cover her sensitive and soft cheeks
People know who she belongs to

Fear s t r e t c h e s her eyes
When she thinks of doing something for
herself
Loving herself
Blasphemy sears her ears more than empty

rhetoric from the pulpits of false teachers
Drowning her in a dunk pool of doubt
With a target worn out from self-esteem
hits
Because Shame's grip has a Hercules grip
on her heart
And doesn't desire
    to let her go

Pride

I don't care what Rick James says.
I am one helluva drug.
My silky serum uses needles of silver
tongue saliva that roughly pierces the thin
outer membrane of flesh and goes on a fast
police chase to your veins.
Quietly I whisper into your blood's ear
everything I want you to hear.
You don't need them.
Don't study others.
You are awesome by yourself.
I ain't fa' dealing with other people's opinions.
Gone somewhere with that.
I penetrate your heart.
Pull on the lever that makes your soul hit
the jackpot and say BINGO!
B-1 asshole
I-4 certain known is
N-7 seconds
G O ing to lose my mind if I can't take your
Attention prisoner.
I arrest your logic for illegal intent to
distribute humbleness.
My shackles caress your slit wrists
compressing the pain of love lost.

Welcome....prepare to be *Scared Straight*.
You spend time in the yard bench-pressing
selfishness gaining muscles of loneliness
with my homies Greed and Envy.
Trying to protect yourself from shanks of
spite and disrespect.
I insert bars into your truth and leave you a
solid rock bed of lies and trouble-filled
toilet faucets closed with concrete chaos.
You lie prostrate looking up
at the ceiling wondering....
Who can I run to? To fill this empty space?
The answer is...no one.
People have moved on from your court
case and battles.
No more #humblepeoplematters.
No more protest and rallies for your sanity.
No more visitation or
money on commissary.
But I snuggle beside you.
My orange jumpsuit is tattered from fist
fights of ended friendships whispering *I,
Pride, love you...we in this thang...forever.*

Silence

I don't like you.
Yet I cannot swipe left to get rid of you.
While the television turns *guided*
by the *light* of the computer,
I sit *young* and *restless* listening to *the world
turn* through music.
Why do you give such drama?
Why do you choose to make easy hard with
a stop that always goes?
I cannot lay down without the matrix
letters in shades of green racing by and me
back bending to avoid them.
I will admit that you and
I were the *serpentine fire* and *fantasy* that
earth, wind, and fire sung about.
I wanted you for the way you caressed my
mind like a stripper pole and hung on for
life as your legs, thighs, ass,
and breasts kept me occupied.
But as I get older, I realize that
I want to be for real.
I want an honest to God relationship with
someone that loves me not just for my body
but for my mind and spirit.
I want someone that I can see a movie or

maybe even see a play on Saturday...
or even maybe roll a tree or feel the breeze
or listen to symphony or maybe chill and
just be like Jill Scott....
Her long walks sound so awesome.
I know you are used to people
being quiet and reserved.
But...I am not the shoe to your
Cinderella wardrobe.
So please, Silence, leave me alone
before the clock strikes twelve.

ADHD

I don't want to talk to you.
You remind me that time slips away faster
than the glass slippers on Cinderella's feet
as she's trying to get home.
Midnight will pass.
Morning will too.
Yet my mind is centered on you.
You are the perfect verse over a tight beat.
The mind reader when I can't speak that
knows exactly how to strike me out of this
game called life.
Every time I'm ready to bat…someone gets
out or goes home or steals third.
Then I'm stuck waiting another inning to
get a bat at greatness.
Please…
Please…
Leave me be.
Give my mind the chance to rise to the
occasion or falter under pressure instead of
just completely keeping me out of the oven.
The heat shows my true almond colors and
turns raw dough into gooey goodness to
the last drop.
I promise you that time awaits soon when

you and I can intertwine our beautifully
manicured hands together.
I will acknowledge your every nudge, your
wet kiss, and your love handles close to my
conscious.
You will have all my attention.
Nothing will be deficit.
For I will be hyper
                        For the disorder
        Of you.

One-Way Mirror

I felt trapped.
I pressed my palm and met cold glass.
I hoped you would hear me if you couldn't
see me.

I felt jealous.
I colored my eyes black every morning so
green couldn't be seen through the glass.
I smiled believing it could save face.

I felt underappreciated.
I screamed in the highest pitch possible to
crack the glass.
I wondered if you knew I was missing.

I felt weak.
I mimicked my hands and body to his
moves in the glass.
I thought you would actually pay attention
to me.

I felt inadequate.
I sat on the floor and just stared at your
beautiful world from the glass.
I knew I would never be him.

The Slip Under My Church Dress

This rectangle provides you with a full
length replicate of yourself.
But…you forgot that you created me after
he was crafted from your image.

You carefully and cautiously took his hand.
The glass became liquid to your touch and
allowed him the chance to cross over to see
the world, make mistakes, lose his heart,
gain a friend, dance a dance, smile a smile,
get a job, sail an ocean, and sleep near you.
But…you forgot me.

My glass barrier kept me from those
precious moments.
It kept me from you.
It keeps me from you.
And I'm waiting for your hand.
I'm waiting for the liquid glass so you can
pull me out into a world anew.

A Coward's Worst Fear

Bravery doesn't know you.
It fears your cowardly lion that guards the
door to your heart.
It yelps at your snail like reflexes to trying
something new.
It shudders at the thought of your yellow
eyes piercing with a dull knife into your
shallow soul.
You wonder why people don't want to take
a swim.
YOU never go out on a limb.
You never give in to your desire to be
different.
Kissing the feet of Teena Marie hoping that
her faith stepping is enough tightrope
walking for your brain to handle with the
stick up its butt and not in hand.
What else can you not do?
What else can you not say?
Aren't your knees tired from knocking like
every supervillain worker bee that leaves
the hive the second they realize that they
might not make it?
Your livers are fed up with planting lilies
that will never flourish into morning glories

or sunflowers.
They fear the dark side of the moon.
Starscream tips his hat to you on your
ability to transform into a hunchback in a
tower with no bell.
You constantly question your strength to
handle Notre Dame…or any lady.
Bravery has mountains to climb,
Words to inspire,
Confidence to implant.
That can't happen to you who can't simply
move,
Simply speak,
Simply feel.

I Carry

I carry my heart on my arm.
Sleeves change when they are dirty.
I carry my heart on my arm,
And flex it when its broken and not strung.

I carry my heart in my eyes.
Cartoons taught me that.
I carry my heart in my eyes,
So I see the pain before it hits me.

I carry my heart between my legs.
Vaginas and penises call the shots.
I carry my heart between my legs,
So when they rub together I am no
longer cold.

I carry my heart in my fingertips.
I know what burns and have a keepsake.
I carry heart in my fingertips,
Because I need to teach my sensitivity
a lesson.

I carry my heart in my breast.
My lungs told me they needed room
to breathe.

The Slip Under My Church Dress

I carry my heart in my breast,
For they give life where 1 lump can
take it away.

I carry my heart in my brain.
They have a love/think relationship.
I carry my heart in my brain,
So my intelligence has a check and balance.

My heart is carried in many places,
Each place plays its part.
I wonder what happens,
When I drop my heart from the start?

Depression

I wish I could see sunny days that sweep
the clouds away.
My air is never sweet.
Never clean.
Palmolive or Ajax couldn't wash away with
thick and pure bubbles the thoughts that
consume my mind.

This is how depression feels.

When you try to appeal to my optimism,
she is resting in an induced coma just so she
can live.
She only breathes so I won't completely die.
The pills won't turn me completely into
Sleeping Beauty's ugly cousin Peaceful
Death.
The rope won't completely asphyxiate me
like Rapunzel on Shampoo day.
The water won't complete fill my lungs that
envies Ariel's abilities to float.
I want…no…I desire a chance to be okay
with a smile's embrace.
Give it the opportunity to douse me with
happiness' pheromones so contentment and

laughter will be attracted to me.
I float like a butterfly and sting like a bee
every second against this formidable
opponent.
Your eyes only see that I don't talk to you.
I leave messages unanswered.
I didn't hold your hand after she broke up
with you.
I forgot your birthday.
I never commented on your Facebook
status.
I'm just...not there.
I've been working on this railroad all the
livelong day trying to get to clarify station
so enjoyment and friendliness can get on
and enjoy the ride.

Attention

What more can I do for you?
How can I do more?
Molecules smaller than salt grains
already worship your feet's shadows.
Fairly visible hairs salute you when your
presence conquers the room.
And I stand there living off of
your every word.
It's what I know and what I live.
Sleepless nights fuel your monster truck
that trample over the triplets: my self-
esteem, my self-confidence, and myself.
The triplets cry in intervals throughout
Nyx's playtime. His touch brings out the
loudest wail to Sound's speakers. And my
ears never fully recover.
And I've tried.
I've prayed.
I've meditated.
I've wondered.
Did I mention I prayed?
Desperately seeking a moment when I
could develop my *Underground Railroad* to
freedom.
I get it.

The Slip Under My Church Dress

You don't consider yourself harmless.
You think you're helpful.
Your parents, Arrogance and Negativity,
did a fantastic job boosting your ego.
But only you think that and your blindness
is far more than Stevie Wonder and
Ray Charles combined.
It paralyzes you from seeing the world
in wretched flames:
High in temperature, conniving in nature,
demeaning in action, and
contagious in representation.
So Shadrach, Meshach, and
Abednego's bravery can't save me.
Ruth's love can't heal me.
Abraham's faith can't comfort me.
Because you have me at your Attention.

She Knows

She knows.
She knows it will hurt me.
More than 1000 needles piercing my side.
More than slamming my finger 20 times in
a car door.
She knows it will hurt me and that is why
her silence is loud.

She knows.
She knows it will lie to me.
More than mirrors in a fun house.
More than husbands who want to please
their wives.
She knows it will lie to me and that is why
her truth hides under her bed.

She knows.
She knows it will destroy me.
More than atomic bombs on Hiroshima and
Nagasaki.
More than Donald Trump's angry tweets.
She knows it will destroy me and that is
why she hesitates pushing the button.

She knows.

She knows it will mislead me.
More than a right arrow gone left.
More than an upward rocket pointing
down.
She knows it will mislead me and that is
why she turned her GPS off.

But with everything she knows,
Knowledge still couldn't protect me from
me.

It

OOOOOOh…

I stare profusely.
Can't take my eyes off it.
I look knowing weakness is evident.

I hear distinctly.
Don't like the melody of it.
I listen intending to be damaged.

I feel repeatedly.
Never prepared for its texture.
I touch believing vulnerability waits for me.

I sniff vigorously.
Not fond of its aroma.
I smell understanding death may occur.
I devour intentionally.
Haven't acquired a stomach for it.
I taste pushing truth out the way.

My senses give in.
Transformation begins.

I know it's wrong to lie.

The Slip Under My Church Dress

I do it profusely.
I know it's wrong to cheat.
I do it distinctly.
I know it's wrong to steal.
I do it repeatedly.
I know it's wrong to backstab.
I do it vigorously.
I know it's wrong to fake.
I do it intentionally.

It may decay you.
It empowers me.
I become the greatest hypocrite.
Your senses will ever meet.

Super Power Silence

I let you cross the line.
The bold white paint warns you
of oncoming traffic.
You believe your body is invincible.
So who am I to argue with Superman?
No one.
Just a lowly human that desires to be
saved from the forces of evil.
But what if that evil force is you?
What if by day you are extremely
extravagant while at night you create evil
in the name of good?
What if radioactive insects inject their
ultra-venom into your bloodstream
so you can leap from building to
building creating chaotic catastrophes
meant to provide putrid problems?
Who am I to attempt rational
and logical emotions?
No one.
Just a friend who knows your secrets
more than I know myself.
I pray for peace.
I desire moments where no signal tattoos
the sky and government agencies are

formed to combat those who believe in
themselves so much that they believe
the world should too.
I know better.
I know your power is poisonous.
But I've kicked myself to the side of silence.

GPS

My thumb points up on a dusty, lonely
highway.
It hopes and prays that it is not treated like
a criminal.
It's innocent,
  its host is not.
I have been stranded here before,
  to my own doing
Forgetting who I am and the power within
my skin,
I peer over my glasses
  Believing the mirage is a reality
  Believing my mistakes are set ups for
greatness,
I am still lost.
I still wander aimlessly through my heart's
desert
  Wishing water would wash my
  insecurities away.
I trek through my rainforests
  Hoping birds can drown my doubt's
voice.
I fly over my mountains and valleys
  Praying oxygen may fill my
  confidence's lungs.

Google Maps and Waze mock me in silence.
They know how to get people where they
need to be.
I wish I could get my identity to arrive at a
destination.

THE EPIPHANY

Life I

I watched Life breathe—
    Inhale excitement,
    Exhale hope.
I watched Life ride—
    Toward adventure,
    On a prayer.
I watched Life eat—
    Consume power,
    Digested control.
I watched Life dance—
    Two steps to the light,
    Two steps to redemption.
I watched Life forgive—
    Bowed in gracefulness,
    Stand in greatness.
I watched Life climb—
    Held on to peace,
    Pushup on strength.

I watched Life procreate —
    Meld with love,
    Thrust with pleasure.
I watched Life live.
Life watched me fall —
    Off of a sofa,
    Pushed by evil.
Life watched me cry —
    Wipe with despair,
    Wet with sadness.
Life watched me carry —
    Burdens of adulthood,
    Weights of dissention.
Life watched me run —
    Away from my passion,
    Into someone's nightmare.
Life watched me cower —
    Away from conflict,
    Against blame.
Life watched me shield —

Blockade honesty,
Deny truth.
Life watched me wither —
Into a dried raisin,
Become a corpse.
Life watched me die.

Life II

Life asked

"Motivation?"

I answered

"Past".

Life asked

"Support?"

I answered

"Some".

Life asked

"Education?"

I answered

"Separation".

Life asked

"Necessities?"

I answered

"Thwarted by Wants".

Life asked

"Nurturing?"

I answered

    "Self-taught".

Life asked

    "Waiting?"

I answered

    "Yes".

Life found the problem.

Life replied

    "Sweetheart.

    Waiting warrants weariness.

        Passion can't live where drive has no road.

        If you are waiting for me as a gift, then your Wait's vainness is winning.

    Find me for yourself.

    Find me in your identity.

    Find me in your actions.

    Find me in your dreams.

    Find me in your heart.

    I am not easy.

Difficulty is my true essence.

Lotus is my favorite flower.

      Slavery is my favorite history lesson.

      Pain is the fire that shaped my clay pot filled with ashes of loss and disappointment.

Yet, I live.

      Daring anyone or thing to deny my right

To

Be

Me."

Secret Weakness

You think I'm unbreakable.
I can sail icy waters between two mounds
of dirt without a single dent or scratch
harming my 46, 328 ton frame.
You are wrong.
While you and yours prance along my top
deck, snuggle comfortably inside the beds
of my cabins and dine gracefully between
my stern and bow...I see the trouble that is
coming ahead.

You think I'm unbreakable.
I win awards, show up to every football
game, and run any club that I am asked to
do.
You are wrong.
And while you and yours check out at 4 PM
and arise at 7 AM, discuss the stupidity of
that student who is SPED, and refuse to
allow anything above a 70 in your class...
I see the trouble that is coming ahead.

Because...I am breakable.

Many others tried to warn you.

Ghosts of ships past whispered *"This is a bad idea…"* as each nail was hammered into my bridge and port hole.
Frozen water has claimed the lives of people and things from places they wanted to go.

Recommendations said that "she is a bit power hungry".
Write ups have my name permanently etched in ink waiting for the next time I put my kids before my position.
I've thrown keys at kids. I'm not stable. At. All.

And still at 11: 40 PM on a chilly Sunday night, I met my fate.
At 3:25 PM on a sunny Tuesday afternoon, I met my match.

And all hope was lost.

The first three hours were Denial's finest moments.
As people plunged and my body cracked, I waited for the King's horses and men to piece me back together.
But Humpty Dumpty's crew was nowhere

to be found in the sea of icebergs and angry
waves.
I eventually relaxed and gave in to the
ocean's strength and smooth, silky sounds.

The first three hours were Anger's favorite
playtime.
Ideas swirled in my brain's cauldron that
could make the Sanderson sisters blush
poison apple red.
Thackery Binx cried from his grave
knowing the evil I was capable of.
I needed something stronger than Hercules
to provide me with Eirene's peaceful
demeanor.

Water is forgiving.
It has a way of comforting you like a care
bear blanket.
The sea barnacles and algae hug my rust
infected interior and make themselves at
home.

Husbands are awesome.
They provide security better than Brinks
would ever be able to afford.
His happiness injects itself without
permission into my depression party of

one.

I'm not sure what History and Future want
from me, and I don't want to know.
Their input has already caused me more
hell than Satan on God's bad day.
I do know that if perfection is what they
want,
What they believe in,
What they think is the perfect match for me.
Then truly History and Future don't know
me at all,
And I refuse to be on water or in a
classroom with ignorant advisors like them.

A Beautiful Wreck

You look so beautiful that it's intimidating.
I know the reason.
Your custom body paint hugs the curves of
your metal frame, distracts my mind, and
seduces Thought's train.
Suddenly, Thought derails and crashes and
burns.
The scene is disgustingly grotesque.
Intelligence's dendrites wiggle and flop like
fish.
Creativity's body is in pieces everywhere.
Bravery starts sneezing and puking up the
faith it ate before the ride.
Thought is sitting on its side…waiting for
help.
And the custom body paint that hugged
your frame dangles for dear life along with
cracks of contempt and dents of depression
and broken glass of guilt.
I want to blame you.
You knew I was hard to stop, packed with
power, moving at a constant speed, headed
for destination…
But I know it's me.
I believed that if we melded together I

could hide in your shadow while you fight
off sun's burns.
Unfortunately, the sun has a way of getting
to everyone wherever you are.
The more I try to run and hide...the more
he tries to bring me to the light.
You probably offer a lot to someone.
That someone is not me.
I know you will find someone who will pay
for your damages and claims.
The question is...how will I pay for my
own since insurance doesn't cover failure?

Love Believed

He was Goliath, but no stone could knock
him down,
No slingshot was strong enough,
And I wasn't tall enough.

He was Superman, but no kryptonite was
powerful enough to tame his strength.
Bullets and knives were slave to his ardor.
I was completely penetrable.

You traveled far and wide,
North and south,
Around the world in 80 days,
Just to get a whiff of his alcoholic stench on
your lips.
I can't get you to move 1 millimeter for me.

So the night when he and tissue paper
became my worst enemy, it's no surprise
that you believed them over me. You
allowed Kleenex and a jheri curl to take
over my world. You wouldn't avenge me
or provide justice.

I was the perfect porridge, but you didn't

believe it.
Any other little girl with curly ringlets had
an open invitation into your heart's home.
I needed 3 proofs of identification.

I was the perfect verse, but you didn't like
the beat.
You rather sell records than purchase
honesty,
And I won't make you a lot of money.

He came clopping in steel toe cowboy boots
and assless chaps busting through rickety
saloon doors.
Each step-a flag for confidence.
Each eyebrow-arched for seriousness.
Each arm-triangular set for a shootout.
You melted like butter on movie popcorn.
I can't get you excited to see a preview of
my excellence.

So the morning when I spilled my guts all
over your altar of assistance, my sacrifice
wasn't enough for you to even
acknowledge. The covenant between
mother and daughter was shattered. My
wilderness continued for forty more years.

I wish…
I wish my eyes could stay half way open.
That moment lifts my eyes every morning
from tumultuous sleep and burns the
darkness of my eyelids.
You purchased a round trip ticket at the
gate when you chose to say *He didn't mean
it. He was just playing.*
You allowed molestation to travel first
class, revel in the perks of my adolescents,
and left a disgusting mess in my youthful
seat.
It had time for me.
It made room for me.
It called me his own and told me that Love
never liked me.
So I never liked Love back.
Rumors kept us apart from each other.
I was too afraid to confront Love and fight
for the right to be in Love's good graces.
But…Love fought for me.

Love
knew what David could do.
savored in Clark Kent's talents.
GPS'd my location.
gave me permission to be me.
enjoyed listening to my melody.

couldn't wait to give me two thumbs up
with a standing ovation.

So while the ghosts of your penises past
have attempted to deconstruct my
Christmas Carol, I'm grateful for Love's
Tiny Tim resilience to believe in my holiday
miracle.

Cloudy

Air.
Water.
You combine to make a pillow for Sky's
bed.
So it can bask in Sun's rays or rest while
thunder preys.

Cluttered.
Hoarded.
Reminders collect to distract a mind from
Responsibility's stare.
So it won't burn a hole or admit truth.

Your consistency amazingly infuriates me.
Your avoidance tactics are studied by US
Representatives and Senators.
Yet you see nothing wrong with your
chaotic purpose.

Grey.
Full.
Condensation has reached his limit and can
no longer win the war against gravity.
Tears of joyous pain drop to earth's
reluctant skin.

Gray.
Consumed.
Memory has taken its last byte of activity
pie.
Space in Brain's computer freezes to control
the alternate deletion.

My patience is pissed with my
Performance's poor acting skills.
My happiness is hopping to the starting
line hoping to hear the gunshots shout
encouragement.
One day, I looked up to you and realized
that you hang out up there to deliver down
here because you can't handle what you
dish out.
But…today is the day I poke a heavy hole
in your puffy space in my life.

So I can see heaven and sanity clearly with
no clouds in sight.

Lotus

Love kisses and hate fists made Dirt and
Water the Sofia and Harpo of the nature
realm.
Their moments of pleasure created the
perfect incubator to a beautiful
roughneck...a roughneck that thought
tough was normal.
Dirt and Water's families came with their
own baggage.
Water's clarity and honesty was as shallow
and cheap as a Dollar Store kiddie pool.
Dirt's reality was as fake as Joan Rivers'
face.
How does such beauty encounter these self-
absorbed elements that have morphed into
a super selfish force of evil in denial?

His eyes opened.
Stamens surrounded his face.
Sun, however, was on his mind and heart.
He watched older cousins, aunts, and
uncles rise to the surface.
Their victory blessed him with small
tendrils of heat across his petals.
He knew there was something special

about that place above him.
He couldn't stop until the sun and him
could play together forever.

Distractions tried to trap him and choke his
motivational spirit.
Ghosts of flowers past laid to his right and
left who's suicidal motivation overcame
their heart's drive for greatness.
Sometimes
       Anger controlled.
       Jealousy consumed.
       Depression called.
But…the sun.
The sun was his prize.
The sun was gold.

Dragonflies and bees buzz "Eye of the
Tiger" to his staples.
He ingested patience and searched for
company that wanted the sun just like he
did.
Some of their petals were different colors,
but he didn't mind.
Moments of discouragement turned into
minutes of delight.
Minutes of delight turned into months of
determination.

He cherished those times.
Dirt and Water were not his end any
more...he had the power.
>   To change the ending.
>   To control the narrative.
>   To connect finally with the
>   victorious perennials who basked in
>   the sun.

I Can...

I can feel the energy
Transforming me
Coursing through my veins because of your
words
Words that are succulent barbeque sauce on
honest ribs
Slowly cooked and tender to Truth's touch

I can desire warmth
Encase myself in the coat of you
Develop your actions, thoughts, and words
in my own way
Words that drip off Dracula's fang
As Satisfaction's liquid representation

I can see the light
Illuminating me
Blinding myself into your shadow
A shadow that follows you and attaches me
to its hip
So it can NEVER be alone

I can know the consequences
Cornering me
In Identity's back alley

Kicking constantly amidst the powerful punches
Because it doesn't want to work, but it wants the rewards

I can decide to run
Farther than Forrest Gump on a thinking day
Wearing the tread out from my changing shoes
Cause the Pacific Ocean will allow me to swim away
From the enticing influence of you.

Gravity

Isaac Newton's head was popped by
Satan's temptation fruit.
He then understood that evil wanted to be
grounded as well.
It wanted a chance to pummel the earth just
like it pummeled life and death.
The duality of Newton's discovery can also
be a saving grace.
When is the question.

> When is it an angel and when is it an
> imp?
> When sweat beads crawl down my
> face with a push up?
> When my ex-boyfriend whispers "I
> rather be with you" in my ear?
> When I'm shoved into a cop car for
> looking suspect in my BMW?
> When I'm excommunicated from
> holiness because my love has a
> vagina like me?

It seems that down is the new up.
The new idea like gravity.
We learned there is a reason for everything,
> A source to each beginning,

A stupid person for each rule,
That makes us have to surrender our
freedom.
More than taken Native American land.
So the apple's trip was more than just
science,
           More than an epiphany,
           More than a revelation,
It sealed the fate that what is elevated must
always descend,
And we fight every day to stay up.

Needs and Wants

You touch is what I need.
It's my water.
The hydrogen and oxygen molecules
infiltrate my skin,
Provide me the vitamins I want and need.
My mouth is silent.
My mind's not pondering.
My body will not move,
So I can endure the compassion of you.

Your adoration is what I need.
It's the secret sauce to my daily meal,
That makes crap, ignorance, and stupidity
retreat to their bunkers,
And wait for Wonder Woman to risk it on
the war field.
Your words are the sheet music.
My mind craves to play,
Regardless of key changes or accidentals.

My silence is my weakness.
It's worse than Everclear
straight with no chaser,
Because I feel undeserving.
I feel remorse.

I feel fear.
To admit that you are a need,
And never a want,
In my world of absolute bliss.

Please

Cliché me PLEASE
      With your addictions
      Your fixes
      Your hits.
And I will tell you that they are not shit
      Compared to mine.
I've had it since I was five.
It was spoon fed to me by aunts and uncles,
Enhanced by church members & school
faculty,
But no doctor saw it.
None could cure.

Tell me PLEASE
      Of your nightmares
      Your headaches
      Your migraines,
And you would think me insane
      Compared to you.
I inhaled my addiction.
I watched me shoot it up my nostrils,
scramble my brain, and dance on my
dendrites.
Nights I couldn't get my fix were sleepless
and long.

Withdrawal was imminent.
Pain was evident.

Humor me PLEASE
      Of your losses
      Your doubts
      Your low self-esteem,
And I would wish for your dreams.
      Compared to mine.
I know nothing of who I really am.
I've been black, white, stuck up, ratchet,
confused, intelligent, efficient, powerful,
depressed, overjoyed, charismatic, and
annoying simultaneously.
But them co-exist peacefully? HA!
Chances fare for lightning to strike twice,
And the person struck to still have life.

Don't tell me
      "Jesus will work it out."
      "I need to quit."
      "It's okay."
      "You don't know what to do"
      "Work through it"
      "Stop"
      "Just pray"

This addiction did not come in one day.

A lot of things led to this point.
To unravel this knot will take time and
effort.
It will take silence and discipline.
It will take a lot.

So relate to me PLEASE
        Of your cares
        Your hopes
        Your aspirations
And I will tell you my work is not done,
        Compared to me
Because my addiction is attention,
        And I can't get away from it because
you keep giving it to me.

Finish

Do you remember the end?
       Was it good?
       Was it bad?
Good endings usually are forgotten.
Bad endings last forever.
Very few remember the end to the Miss
USA pageant.
People wish they could forget 9/11/2001.
That's why I stop
       Seal up the moment
       Think of other options
       Open up something new
       Pursue a new route
So loose ends hug me like cellulite on too
small swimsuits.
They follow me — cautiously meandering —
just so I can't keep a pace.
I wonder however how a finish could feel.
       Would I run in slow motion through
a ribbon?
       Jump into the arms of my true love
to engage in a kiss that lasts forever?
       Find my long lost sister and play
patty cake in the sunset?
Or would their just be silence?

If so

     I need no ribbon.

     True love doesn't exist.

     I don't like meeting family members.

Let me stop before I cross the line.

Let me avoid the congratulations and celebrations.

Let me be still in the mystery to unfold from not experiencing THE END.

Special Acknowledgements

Ebon Bush and T & J Media: You are the greatest husband/cheerleader a girl like me could have. I don't deserve you, but thanks be to God for His grace.

Jeremy Neal and Martin Denesse: Thank you for assisting me in protecting my words. You guard my heart like it's your own.

Christian Starr and Archon Editing & Reviewing: You are the greatest editor in this life and the next! Thank you for always pushing me beyond my own limits.

SITES Poetry Club: My babies! You all remind me every day how much I love teaching. I'm ready for the future because you all are it! Thank you for all the love and encouragement.

Ashlee Johnson-Savoy, Miriam Morgan, and Danielle Doucet: My FIRST writing partners! Thank you for never letting me go despite my actions or thoughts.

Dr. Leslie Cappiello: Thank you for "unleashing the dragon".

Pen2Pad Ink: Thank you for your constant love and support through this process. Your consistent hugs and advice through this process has me eternally in your debt. Let's make awesomeness!

About the Author

"I am a person's worst nightmare in a daydream. I speak loudly but eloquently. You do not want me around, but you need me. I am a queen of many trades with minors in certain abilities. I am the friend whose arms you can die in. I am the love that may speak conditionally but is unconditional in giving. My passion in love is just as adamant as my passion in anger. I refuse to cut one short for the other to live. I am what I say I am. I have spoken."

- J. W. Bella

J. W. Bella is a product of Louisiana

swamps and good food who transplanted into Texas' opportunities and love for everything bigger. She's been a writer for over 15 years since her first introduction to poetry in her seventh grade gifted class. Currently, she's a high school English teacher in Irving, Texas and sponsors a poetry club that helps teens write and express themselves through written and performance poetry.

Poetry has saved her from death and life thanks to a pen, some very powerful words, a lot of tears, many ripped papers, regrets, joys, and love. She's forever grateful for her gift and hopes that others will be saved as well.

Get connected with
Author J.W. Bella on social media

 JW Bella

 jwbellawrites

 jwbellawrites